A BULLY-FREE SCHOOL

A BULLY-FREE WORLD

Text by Pamela Hall
Illustrations by Bob Ostrom

magic wagon

Content Consultant
Finessa Ferrell, Director,
National Center for School Engagement

visit us at www.abdopublishing.com

Published by Magic Wagon, a division of the ABDO Group, PO Box 398166, Minneapolis, MN 55439. Copyright © 2013 by Abdo Consulting Group, Inc. International copyrights reserved in all countries. All rights reserved. No part of this book may be reproduced in any form without written permission from the publisher.

Looking Glass Library™ is a trademark and logo of Magic Wagon.

Printed in the United States of America, North Mankato, Minnesota.
032012
112012

 THIS BOOK CONTAINS AT LEAST 10% RECYCLED MATERIALS.

Text by Pamela Hall
Illustrations by Bob Ostrom
Edited by Holly Saari
Design and production by Craig Hinton

Library of Congress Cataloging-in-Publication Data
Hall, Pamela, 1961-
  A bully-free school / by Pamela Hall ; illustrated by Bob Ostrom.
      p. cm. -- (A bully-free world)
  ISBN 978-1-61641-847-2
  1. Bullying in schools--Juvenile literature. 2. Bullying--Prevention--Juvenile literature.
I. Ostrom, Bob, ill. II. Title.
  LB3013.3.H33 2013
  371.5'8--dc23
                          2011038554

TABLE OF CONTENTS

BULLYING
AT SCHOOL

Why do kids bully? One reason is because bullies need to have power over others. Bullies pick on kids they think are weaker. They try to make others feel bad about themselves. Then bullies feel better than the kids they pick on.

Bullying happens at school because there are many kids around. Bullies can bully in the library, in the hallway, or at lunch. Bullying is not okay! Everyone can do his or her part to stop it. The kids at Niceville Elementary School are bullying each other. Let's see how they fix their bad behavior and make their school bully-free!

RUMORS

Social bullying is spreading rumors or leaving people out on purpose. People who spread rumors say mean things they know will hurt someone's feelings. Social bullying can hurt more than a kick or a punch.

WHAT TO DO

Sarah is spreading a rumor about Carlos. Rumors are stopped in two main ways. One way to stop a rumor is to tell the bully to knock it off. Carlos can tell Sarah, "You don't know what you are talking about." Making Sarah feel uncool helps make her stop bullying.

A second way to stop a rumor is to turn it into a joke. But, Carlos should only make a joke if he is okay with it.

PEER PRESSURE

Kids like to do what other kids are doing. Emily tells Lee she shouldn't invite Isabel to Lee's party. Emily says she won't go unless Lee does this. That is called peer pressure. This type of bullying makes Isabel feel sad and hurt.

WHAT TO DO

The best thing for Isabel to do is to talk to kids in other classes. She should meet other kids at recess. Finding a new group of friends shows Emily and Lee that they can't bother Isabel. That takes away their power. They will stop bullying Isabel once they see she doesn't care what they do.

NAME-CALLING

Mean words hurt a lot. Verbal bullies say things they know will hurt others. Some bullies say, "Nobody likes you." They might say, "You are ugly." This makes them feel better than everyone else.

Taylor is teasing Joe and calling him names. Ava hears this. She knows it's not right. But how can she help Joe?

15

WHAT TO DO

Ava can stand up for Joe! She learned nine out of ten kids in elementary school have been bullied at least once. She needs to do her part to stop bullying.

Ava looks Taylor right in the eye. She tells him to stop teasing Joe. She is firm. Ava makes Taylor look silly instead of strong.

HITTING AND SHOVING

Derek is a physical bully. He says he will hurt Tim. Derek makes Tim do things Tim doesn't want to do. Derek takes Tim's things, too. Physical bullying is very scary. Tim is afraid.

19

WHAT TO DO

About 20 percent of elementary schools say bullying is a problem. That is still too much! What can Tim do?

First, Tim shouldn't be in a place where Derek can find him alone. Tim needs to walk home with someone he trusts. Second, Tim needs to tell an adult he trusts. This is very important if he can't get away from Derek. Telling an adult is not tattling. It is reporting. The adult will help keep Tim safe.

21

TAKE THE
BULLY TEST

How can you tell if you ever bully? You are a bully if you do things you know will hurt people or make them feel bad. Ask yourself these questions:

- Do I feel better when I hurt other kids or take their stuff?

- Do I use my strength or size to get my way?

- Do I like to leave others out to make them feel bad?

- Have I ever spread a rumor that I knew was not true?

- Do I like teasing others?

Q Is it funny to me when I see other kids getting made fun of?

Q Have I ever kicked, punched, or hit someone?

If you answered "yes" to any of these questions, you might be a bully. Is that really how you want to be?

Of course not! Everyone makes mistakes. You can change the way you act. The first step is to say, "I'm sorry." Practice being nice to other people. Think before you say or do something. Treat others the way you want to be treated.

NOTE TO PARENTS AND CAREGIVERS

Young children often imitate their parents' or caregivers' behaviors. If you show bullying actions or use bullying language, it is likely your children will, too. They do not know their behavior is unacceptable because they see it in trusted adults. You can help prevent your student from bullying by modeling good behavior.

WORDS TO KNOW

peer pressure—a feeling that you must act in the same way as others in order for them to like you.

physical bullying—pushing, kicking, hitting, or touching someone in a harmful way.

reporting—telling an adult about being bullied.

rumor—talk that may not be true but is repeated by many people.

social bullying—telling secrets, spreading rumors, giving mean looks, and leaving kids out on purpose.

verbal bullying—being mean to someone using words, such as by name-calling.

WEB SITES

To learn more about bullying at school, visit ABDO Group online at **www.abdopublishing.com**. Web sites about bullying at school are featured on our Book Links page. These links are routinely monitored and updated to provide the most current information available.